Solomon

Scripture text from
The Contemporary English Version

Master Books

The Wisdom of Solomon

Collection,
Studies of Devotion
(around 1371-1378)
Solomon Enthroned
(137/1687 folio 109r)

This medieval Gothic miniature with its vivid colors presents the crowning of King Solomon. The effect of the scene's balanced composition around the central character of Solomon is reinforced by the use of two colors. The exaggerated size of the king and his throne in relation to the figures surrounding the throne symbolizes the king's greatness.
It is interesting to note that in the symbols of royalty – the crown, the scepter and the long cloak – Solomon is presented as a king of the Medieval Merovingian (Frankish) dynasty.

© Giraudon-Museum Conde, Chantilly (France)

The Son of David

Archaeological site in Egypt

Lying on his bed in the royal palace, King David is near death. A short distance away, down in the valley, his son Solomon* is declared king. As it happens, luck is on the young king's side. He has everything he needs to succeed. The kingdom he inherits is vast, and peace rules on the borders. The large neighboring kingdoms are weak, and the nation's treasury is full.

During his long reign, Solomon will launch major building projects. He will reorganize the kingdom into twelve municipalities, increase the number of scribes in the court, and maintain good relations with his neighbors. He will marry the daughter of the King of Egypt and build strong ties with the King of Tyre in Lebanon. He will become widely respected for his wisdom. The son who follows the great warrior King David will be a wise and peace-making king.**

Allegory of justice on the façade of the Roman courthouse (Italy)

A Heart Full of Good Judgment

The Bible frequently refers to Solomon's extraordinary wisdom. The Bible tells how, at the beginning of his reign, Solomon asked God: *"Please make me wise and teach me the difference between right and wrong"* (1 Kings 3.9). The story of Solomon's difficult decision involving two mothers claiming the same child as her own (see the next page) is an example of how King Solomon was gifted with "the wisdom of God to make fair decisions."

* Solomon
In Hebrew, the name Solomon is connected to the Hebrew word "Shalom," meaning "peace." The very name of the king points to his peaceful rule and time of prosperity for Israel.

** A wise and peace-making king
According to the Bible, King Solomon ruled for about forty years, from 970-931 B.C., almost three thousand years ago.

3

Solomon Makes a Difficult Decision

1 Kings 3.16-28 (excerpts)

One day two women came to King Solomon, and one of them said:

Your Majesty, this woman and I live in the same house. Not long ago my baby was born at home, and three days later her baby was born. Nobody else was there with us.

One night while we were all asleep, she rolled over on her baby and he died. Then while I was still asleep, she got up and took my son out of my bed. She put him in her bed, then she put her dead baby next to me.

In the morning when I got up to feed my son, I saw that he was dead. But when I looked at him in the light, I knew he wasn't my son.

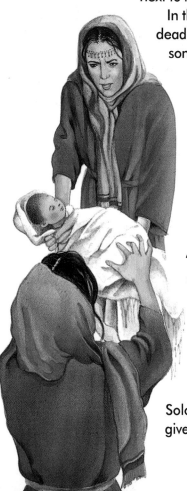

"No!" the other woman shouted. "He was your son. My baby is alive!"

"The dead baby is yours," the first woman yelled. "Mine is alive!"

They argued back and forth in front of Solomon, until finally he said, "Both of you say this live baby is yours. Someone bring me a sword."

A sword was brought, and Solomon ordered, "Cut the baby in half! That way each of you can have part of him."

"Please don't kill my son," the baby's mother screamed. "Your Majesty, I love him very much, but give him to her. Just don't kill him."

The other woman shouted, "Go ahead and cut him in half. Then neither of us will have the baby."

Solomon said, "Don't kill the baby." Then he pointed to the first woman, "She is the real mother. Give the baby to her."

Everyone in Israel was amazed when they heard how Solomon had made his decision. They realized that God had given him wisdom to judge fairly.

Came to King Solomon

During Solomon's time, any victim of injustice could come before the king in search of justice.

Just Don't Kill Him

The true mother thinks of her baby first. She wants him to live. The false mother thinks of herself first. She wants to be right.

Everyone in Israel

This story was told everywhere in the country to show the capacity of Solomon to judge with wisdom.

The Wisdom of Solomon

Wise Persons

People who are wise refuse to believe that they are above or better than others. They think before acting or speaking. All opinions are important to them, so they listen to everyone before making a decision. They remain humble and simple even when others look to them as leaders. They recognize their own weakness and capacity for failing. They keep their promises. They do not try to dominate but only to serve.

Full of Good Judgment

Before taking action or when facing a critical situation, wise people ask themselves, "Where is the good? Where is the evil?" Realizing that evil is sometimes camouflaged in bright-sounding words and plans, they feel responsible to sort through to find the truth. They understand that good is not always immediately visible. They try to see clearly into their own and others' motives. To distinguish between good and evil, persons of wisdom rely on God to enlighten and guide them.

Justice

People who are truly wise do not put all their faith in appearances. They do not make quick judgments but try first to listen to all sides. They do their best to be impartial. To them, each person, whether poor or rich, powerful or voiceless, has rights and responsibilities deserving of respect. They see everyone as equal before the law. They make certain that people do not act only for their own advantage to the detriment of others. Wise persons try to be just and fair.

Friendly

Persons who have acquired wisdom look upon the people who cross their path with kindness. They wish others well and try to establish positive relations with them. They don't set out to criticize or attack. They approach everyone with a spirit of helpfulness and respect. Their first response is to give everyone the benefit of the doubt. Rather than rejecting people, they welcome them and offer whatever help they can. They are truly friendly!

Peacemakers

Peacemakers are wise,
using God's wisdom
to settle disputes.
They refuse to tolerate
the hate that springs
from the heart of one
who rejects God's laws
and guide for living.

They believe in communication.
They are always ready
to find a solution that
maintains harmony and
order in the world. For
them, God is the peacemaker.

Peacemakers react to
situations based on love
and justice from God.

Solomon, in his writings,
understood that peace is
kept when the people bow
to God and love his mercy.
This heart attitude helps
peace spread.

Peacemakers never think
of themselves; only of others
who are suffering injustice.

Such are the peacemakers,
the truly wise.
Blessed are they!

The Temple of Solomon

Jean Foquet, a fifteenth century painter, sets the building of the Temple in Jerusalem within his own time period. In fact, the artist presents the ancient building where the Sacred Chest was housed in what resembles a gothic cathedral. He uses the complementary colors blue and orange to add intensity to his painting as well as to create effective systems of perspective. A master observer of detail, the painter reveals his special talent for presenting crowds and scenes from daily life. His gifts for dramatic use of perspective and realistic re-creation of his times make Jean Foquet the most important French painter of the fifteenth century.

Jean Fouquet (around 1420-1481), Joseph Flavius: *Judaic Antiquities. Construction of the Temple of Jerusalem by the Order of King Solomon* (ms. fr.247 fol.163)

© Telarci-Giraudon - National Library of France, Paris (France)

A Huge Construction Zone

Construction of a basilica model, Museum of the Tower of David, Jerusalem

A few years after Solomon became king, Israel is transformed into a huge construction zone.

The first goal of the new king is to build a magnificent Temple in Jerusalem. Tens of thousands of builders and craftsmen work seven years to complete it.

But Solomon is not content with just the Temple; he decides to build himself a huge palace. According to 1 Kings 7.1-12, he has Forest Hall* built, as well as Pillar Hall, Justice Hall, his own living quarters, and a palace for his wife, the daughter of the King of Egypt. After that, construction begins on gardens, tanks, aqueducts, fortified cities, and stables for the army horses.

Parade in Chichicastenango (Guatemala)

The House of God

For centuries the Jerusalem Temple that Solomon built will be the religious center of Israel. Every day priests sacrifice animals to God on its altars. During important celebrations, like Passover, Pentecost, and the Festival of Shelters, thousands of worshipers flood to the Temple to make their own offerings to God. It is a sacred place ** to every person in Israel, "the place where God is worshiped."

When going to Jerusalem, many people remember Solomon who built the Temple. But few people remember the thousands of workers who were enslaved in its construction. The Bible does not forget them (see the next page).

* Forest Hall
Forest Hall is the largest room in Solomon's palace. It was lined with cedar from Lebanon and had cedar pillars that held up cedar beams. This Hall is part of the royal palace complex and was adjacent to Pillar Hall and Justice Hall.

** Sacred place
In the Temple there was no statue of God, but the Sacred Chest stood for the throne of God. The Sacred Chest held the two flat stones with the Ten Commandments written on them. The Chest symbolized God being among the people of Israel.

The Construction of the Temple

1 Kings 5.13-18; 8.1,2,10-13 (excerpts)

Solomon ordered thirty thousand people from all over Israel to cut logs for the temple…. Solomon divided them into three groups of ten thousand. Each group worked one month in Lebanon and had two months off at home.

He also had eighty thousand workers to cut stone in the hill country of Israel, seventy thousand workers to carry the stones, and over three thousand assistants to keep track of the work and to supervise the workers.

He ordered the workers to cut and shape large blocks of good stone for the foundation of the temple.

Solomon's and Hiram's men worked with men from the city of Gebal, and together they got the stones and logs ready for the temple.

… Solomon decided to have the chest moved to the temple while everyone was in Jerusalem, celebrating the Festival of Shelters….

Suddenly a cloud filled the temple as the priests were leaving the most holy place. The LORD's glory was in the cloud, and the light from it was so bright that the priests could not stay inside to do their work. Then Solomon prayed:

"Our LORD, you said that you
  would live in a dark cloud.
Now I have built a glorious temple
  where you can live forever."

The Drudgery

The tasks of the construction workers were very difficult. They had to travel to Lebanon to find wood and work in quarries hewing stone. They had to transport the huge slabs to the Temple site and then lift them into position.

For the Temple

At the end of this book (page 35) you will find a description of the Temple of Solomon as it is described in the Book of Kings.

A Cloud

Clouds were seen as a sign of the mysterious and glorious presence of God.

A Time To Build

Construction Zones

People set up "construction zones" in an effort to build connections with others and to practice sharing and reciprocity. They work in such zones as medicine, education, and scientific research. They work in the zones of respect, fairness, and human rights. God entrusts to us the task of transforming the earth into an enormous house, welcoming everyone as family.

The House of God

"Houses of God" are places where believers gather to pray and sing together of their faith in God and in God's Word. Carefully built, these houses are signs that remind us of God's presence among us. Through the beauty of church architecture, religious art, color, and music, we express the happiness of believing in God.

God's Temple

God doesn't live in church buildings, synagogues, or any other dwellings we may construct. Nothing can enclose God, who made the universe and everything in it. God is present wherever people gather in his name, to worship, pray, and experience the joy of following Christ. Whenever his people dance for joy or sing for gladness, God is there. God is the good Father who dwells in the hearts of those who love him. He says that nothing can separate his children from his love.

Drudgery

Everyone knows that there are still places on earth where human beings are exploited, underpaid, and treated like slaves. Those places are controlled by people who hate, steal, and lie. God promises that one day he will bring to us a new, eternal city of love. The New Jerusalem is our great hope!

Builders

We spread the
Gospel, in order
to build hope.

We spread the
Bible's message
to build faith.

We speak the
name of Jesus
to build compassion.

We print Bibles
to share God's love
with a hurting world
and build fellowship.

We see the nations
without faith and
we build churches.

We love the truth
of God's laws
and share them
to build trust.

We tell the little
children that Jesus
died for them, and
so we build joy.

Builders,
that is our name!

The Prayer of Solomon

Tiepolo, an eighteenth century artist, shows King Solomon crowned in great splendor and majesty. From the painter Freeness (sixteenth century), this artist borrows showy costumes and plays with light and shadow to lend dignity to the scene. He shows vivid imagination in employing lions symbolically, and he makes bold use of the artistic technique of foreshortening in creating inventive gestures and movements in the characters. Gifted with a refined sense of color, and loving movement and display, Tiepolo is the last of the great Italian baroque (ornate) decorators.

Giovanni Battista or **Giambattista Tiepolo** (school), (1696-1770). *The Queen of Sheba before King Solomon.* Detail: "King Solomon on his Throne."

© Camera Photo-Giraudon-Palazzo Ducale, Venice (Italy)

14

The Prayer of the King

Women and Children Singing, Relief kept in Buenos Aires (Argentina)

The dedication of the Temple in Jerusalem probably took place around 960 B.C. The crowd gathered on the steps of the Temple for the occasion. King Solomon blessed the new dwelling of the Lord and explained why he had built the Temple. His dedication prayer on behalf of the people of Israel included asking the Lord for peace, good harvests, healing from sickness, and the forgiveness of sins.

The Prayer of the People

For many years after Solomon died, people went annually to the Temple in Jerusalem to pray and offer sacrifice to the Lord. They sing: *"It made me glad to hear them say, 'Let us go to the house of the Lord'"* (Psalms 122.1). They come with their joys and their sorrows. Their prayer is a continuation of Solomon's because it expresses their own agony. Solomon's dedication prayer (on the following page) brings together the cries of thousands of women, men, and children of Israel. But it also includes two new discoveries about God:

1. God's dwelling is not only in the Temple.*
2. Even foreigners are called to know God.**

Parade of Young Women in Traditional Costumes in Valencia (Spain)

* Not only in the Temple
Four centuries after Solomon (in 586 B.C.), the Temple will be destroyed by King Nebuchadnezzar of Babylonia and the people taken as captives to Babylonia. It is then that Israel begins to understand more fully that God can be found beyond the walls of the Temple.

** Even foreigners can know God
The Temple was first constructed as the place for Israelites to worship the Lord their God.

B i b l e

When They Will Come To Pray

1 Kings 8.22-43 (excerpts)

Solomon stood facing the altar with everyone standing behind him. Then he lifted his arms toward heaven and prayed:

LORD God of Israel, no other god in heaven or on earth is like you!...

There's not enough room in all of heaven for you, LORD God. How could you possibly live on earth in this temple I have built? But I ask you to answer my prayer. This is the temple where you have chosen to be worshiped.... Whenever any of us look toward this temple and pray, answer from your home in heaven and forgive our sins....

Suppose your people Israel sin against you, and then an enemy defeats them. If they come to this temple and beg for forgiveness, listen from your home in heaven. Forgive them and bring them back to the land you gave their ancestors.

Suppose your people sin against you, and you punish them by holding back the rain. If they turn toward this temple and pray in your name ... please send rain on the land you promised them forever.

Sometimes the crops may dry up or rot or be eaten by locusts or grasshoppers, and your people will be starving. Sometimes enemies may surround their towns, or your people will become sick with deadly diseases. Listen when anyone in Israel truly feels sorry and sincerely prays with arms lifted toward your temple... From your home in heaven answer their prayers, according to the way they live and what is in their hearts....

Foreigners will hear about you and your mighty power, and some of them will come to live among your people Israel. If any of them pray toward this temple, listen from your home in heaven and answer their prayers. Then everyone on earth will worship you, just like your people Israel, and they will know that I have built this temple to honor you.

Not Enough Room in All of Heaven

Today we say "God of the universe." God is "larger" than the Temple and all the universe.

Bring Them Back

Several centuries after Solomon (in 587 B.C.), a portion of the people will be exiled to Babylon and, upon their return to Jerusalem, will rebuild the Temple.

Foreigners

During the exile in Babylon, the Israelites learn to understand better the foreigners among whom they live. They also better understood that the God of Israel is the God of the entire human race.

Today

Turning toward God

Praying

Praying can be described as seeking God and standing reverently in God's presence. Praying consists of opening one's heart to God and speaking trustfully. "Look, Lord! It's me, with my fears and my dreams, with my laughter and my tears! Near to you, I feel protected." Praying is having a confident attitude. The person who prays counts on God.

Praying Together

When believers get together to pray, they form a praying people. They are like a group of children from the same family speaking together in a family council. They remember the word of Jesus, "Whenever two or three of you come together in my name, I am there with you" (Matthew 18.20).

Out-stretched Hands

Body language reflects the prayer uttered in the heart. So many people pray with outstretched hands or bowed heads to show obedience. With such gestures, praying people show themselves poor and weak. Their empty hands symbolize their dependence on God's love, "In my hands, Lord, place your love! Help me then to pass it along to others."

God Listens

Every prayer that comes from a sincere heart reaches God, just as a good parent is sensitive to the needs of a child. We can affirm that God always listens! No cry directed to God is ignored.

Important Prayer

Standing before you, Lord,
here we are with waiting hearts
and extended hands!
We come to give you
our land!

We ask that it remain beautiful
with its autumn colors,
with its springtime bouquets,
with its winter ice crystals,
with its summer fruits.
Don't permit us,
either through our greed or lack of conscience,
to strip it or pollute it.

Look at our land, Lord,
it is so rich and nourishing!
Watch over the fields
so that they are equitably divided
and each person can
taste the harvests and the bread.

Look at our land, Lord,
it is so vast and welcoming!
Watch over it so that
we always allow space
for our foreign and outcast brothers
and sisters.

Before you, Lord,
here we are together
with out-stretched hands
and waiting hearts.
Give us strength and courage
to watch over this gift
you have given
so that it remains a place
where all children,
without exception,
can daily taste
the joy of living!

CHAPTER • 4

The Glory of Solomon

Anonymous, contemporary twentieth century, Ethiopia, *History of the Queen of Sheba*. The wealth of Solomon, exchange of gifts of ivory, gold and a lion.

This Ethiopian miniature, with its vivid colors, presents the meeting between the Queen of Sheba and King Solomon. At the time, royalty exchanged gifts when making official visits. In this scene, the Queen of Sheba offers King Solomon a lion, gold, and ivory. The characters are presented in a simple manner, but the artist uses the exchange of glances to lend dignity to the scene.

The Grandeur of Solomon

The Meeting of the Queen of Sheba and King Solomon, Museum of the Tower of David, Jerusalem

Solomon is considered one of Israel's great kings whose rule includes several accomplishments. First of all, there are his many building projects, the most celebrated of which is the Temple in Jerusalem. But Solomon also builds a fleet of ships and equips his army with chariots and horses. He increases trade with neighboring nations, as well as with distant countries.* He had an eye for details. For example, the six-step throne he built is decorated with the heads of bulls and lions, and the walls of the Temple are adorned with carvings of palm trees and flowers. The Bible characterizes Solomon's rule with these rules: "*While he was king, there was silver everywhere in Jerusalem, and cedar was as common as ordinary sycamore trees in the foothills*" (1 Kings 10.27).

Six-step throne preserved at the Museum of Cairo (Egypt)

The Fame of Solomon

A boat on the Nile (Egypt)

The fame of Solomon continues to spread long after his death. He is seen as the one who introduced wisdom to Israel. His name is connected to many biblical writings, including the books of Proverbs, Ecclesiastes, Song of Songs. We speak of the wisdom of Solomon just as we do of the psalms of David and the Law of Moses. The story of the foreign Queen of Sheba's visit to Solomon shows how widely the wisdom and wealth of the "*sun king*" of Israel were recognized. (See the following page.)

* Neighboring and distant countries
The northern countries Solomon traded with included Lebanon and the people living in modern-day Turkey. To the south, he dealt with the regions around the Red Sea, Arabia and Egypt.

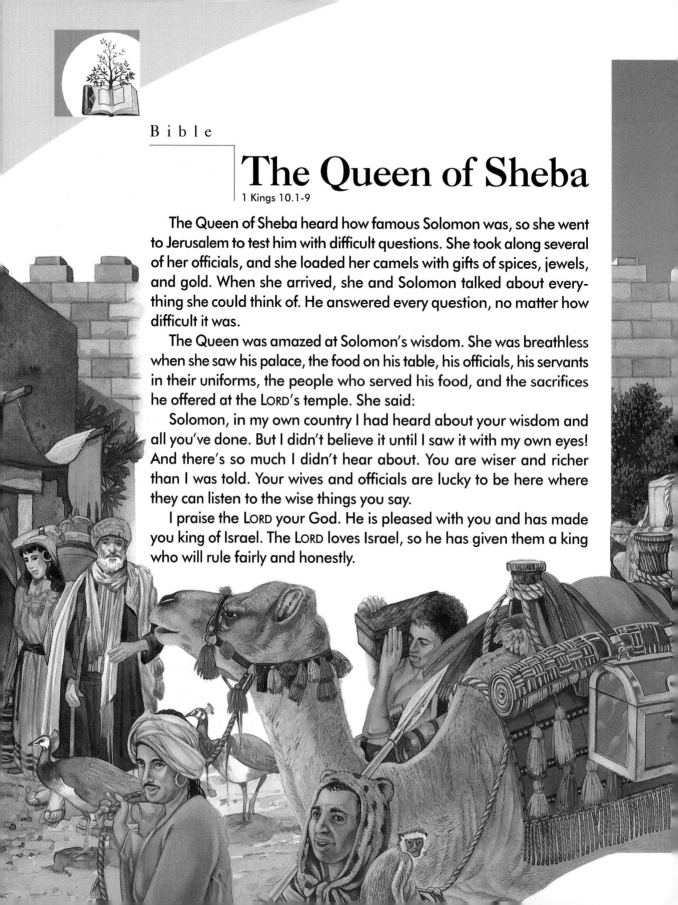

The Queen of Sheba

1 Kings 10.1-9

The Queen of Sheba heard how famous Solomon was, so she went to Jerusalem to test him with difficult questions. She took along several of her officials, and she loaded her camels with gifts of spices, jewels, and gold. When she arrived, she and Solomon talked about everything she could think of. He answered every question, no matter how difficult it was.

The Queen was amazed at Solomon's wisdom. She was breathless when she saw his palace, the food on his table, his officials, his servants in their uniforms, the people who served his food, and the sacrifices he offered at the Lord's temple. She said:

Solomon, in my own country I had heard about your wisdom and all you've done. But I didn't believe it until I saw it with my own eyes! And there's so much I didn't hear about. You are wiser and richer than I was told. Your wives and officials are lucky to be here where they can listen to the wise things you say.

I praise the Lord your God. He is pleased with you and has made you king of Israel. The Lord loves Israel, so he has given them a king who will rule fairly and honestly.

Sheba

The kingdom of Sheba stretched all the way to the south of Arabia. The queen of this country came from very far away.

Difficult Questions

The king and queen engage in a kind of game. She asks him questions (riddles), waiting to see whether Solomon can answer them.

Wiser and Richer

The wisdom of Solomon was larger than the wisdom of all the sons of the Orient and all the wisdom of Egypt (1 Kings 4.30, 31).

Grandeur and Responsibility

Works of Art

God has blessed each of us with imagination and talents, so we are able to sculpt stone and metal, build with wood, write poems, or paint with vivid colors and detail. Artists create the beauty that brings us joy and gives us, in turn, the desire to become creators of beauty in word and action!

Wealth

To be truly wealthy does not consist only in acquiring a great deal of money. There are innumerable and different sources of wealth: having enough food, living in adequate shelter, putting one's intellectual capabilities to work, enjoying freedom and justice, knowing how to read and write, being able to analyze works of art, having friends and family, listening to the music of nature, being in good health – all these are wealth given not for ourselves alone, but to be shared with others.

Responsibilities of the Wealthy

Some individuals and nations possess more financial wealth than others. They are fortunate to have more than enough. However, those same people who are blessed with such wealth have an obligation to be more attentive to the poor, to empower them and others to free them from the bonds of poverty. To be wealthy is truly a great fortune, but it is also a responsibility.

Responsibilities of Government Officials

Being a president, a delegate, a leader, or an elected official is not primarily a private privilege or a source of personal glory. A call to govern is a call to exercise leadership. For those judged capable of assuming this role, it carries the responsibility of giving of time, knowledge, and energy to enact laws and do whatever is necessary to establish justice in society.

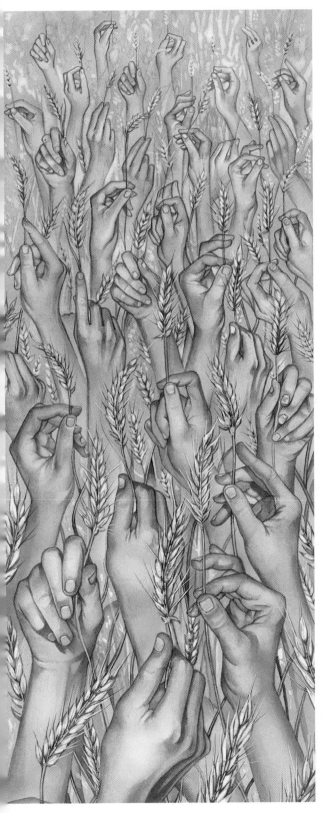

Glory

This glory is modest.
It does not look to shout
from rooftops
its mighty accomplishments
or marvels!

This glory is discreet:
It resides
in bringing help to others,
in offering consolation,
in sharing wealth,
in distributing smiles,
in granting forgiveness!

This glory is simple.
It flourishes in the humble gestures
of everyday accomplishments –
deeds done for the happiness of the
neighbor!

This glory is hidden.
It is brought to light
in the practice of the Gospel
and in the keen attentiveness
to the word of God
urging each human being
to give the best of themselves
so that the earth
becomes one huge
garden of solidarity!

CHAPTER • 5

The Shadows of the Reign

King Rehoboam, detail of a wood ceiling in the St. Martin Church in Switzerland (1130/1140)

In this work, the artist uses transparent colors to give the painting a certain lightness. King Rehoboam is presented on his throne in the manner of the kings of the Medieval Merovingian dynasty and in a very detailed palace setting. The knife he holds is a symbol of his terrible cruelty toward his people. Two shields show the political division that gave birth to two separate kingdoms: Israel in the north, under King Jeroboam, and Judah in the south, ruled by King Rehoboam.

© AKG Photos, Paris (France)

Taxes and Drudgery

A coin repository hidden in a large block of stone

To pay for his grand construction projects and make his fame known, Solomon needs money. The resources left him by his father David are quickly used up. So Solomon imposes taxes on his people. Each of his twelve districts is obligated to supply the palace one month a year. The peasants must deliver wheat, barley, wine, and oil.

In addition to these taxes, first the Canaanites and then the Israelites are forced into slave labor. They are forced to transport wood and stone under the direction of appointed Israelite overseers.*

A woman carrying reeds (Peru)

Rebellion Rumbles

Two men squabbling

During the construction projects undertaken by King Solomon, workers hired from the North are led by a man named Jeroboam to rise up in rebellion.** The uprising is repressed, and Jeroboam is forced to escape to Egypt. Peace reigns as long as Solomon is alive. However, upon his death, the ten northern tribes again ask King Rehoboam to lessen the workload. Will he listen to them? If not, the vast kingdom of Solomon is threatened with division.

* Israelite overseers
Several centuries earlier, the Israelites had been oppressed by the king of Egypt. Now they experience oppression at the hands of their own king.

** Workers hired from the North
This refers to the workers coming from the ten northern tribes who are forced to work at the building sites of Jerusalem located in southern Israel.

B i b l e

The Division of the Kingdom

1 Kings 12.1-19 (excerpts)

Rehoboam went to Shechem where everyone was waiting to crown him king.

… Then together they went to Rehoboam and said, "Your father Solomon forced us to work very hard. But if you make our work easier, we will serve you and do whatever you ask.

"Give me three days to think about it," Rehoboam replied, "then come back for my answer." So the people left….

Three days later, Jeroboam and the others came back. Rehoboam…. spoke bluntly and told them exactly what his own advisors had suggested: "My father made you work hard, but I'll make you work even harder. He punished you with whips, but I'll use whips with pieces of sharp metal!"

When the people realized that Rehoboam would not listen to them, they shouted: "We don't have to be loyal to David's family. We can do what we want. Come on, people of Israel!"…

Ever since that day, the people of Israel have opposed David's family in Judah. All of this happened just as the LORD's prophet Ahijah had told Jeroboam.

David's Family

This refers to the dynasty of David – Solomon, Rehoboam and their successors. They will rule in Jerusalem.

Israel

From this point forward the kingdom is divided in two – the Kingdom of the North called "Israel", with its ten tribes, and the Kingdom of the South called "Judah", with its two tribes.

Ahijah

The prophet Ahijah announces the division of the kingdom of Solomon as a punishment for the disloyalty of the king toward the LORD. Ahijah cuts his coat into ten pieces and gives it to the new king of the North, Jeroboam. Through this gesture, the prophet wants to show that the LORD had taken ten tribes of the kingdom of Solomon (1 Kings 11.30).

The Times of Injustice

Yokes

A yoke is a wooden frame placed on the shoulders of an animal to pull a heavy load or plow. In ancient times, conquerors placed a bar over the shoulders of the people they had defeated to force them to walk hunched over with their heads bent in humiliation. Many, many people today are still forced to live under the yokes of hunger, poverty, and oppression!

The Lure of Power

Given a little power, people are often tempted to act like tyrants. We have evidence of this all around — as leaders of countries or groups of people, and even within families and friends. Relying on their own authority, those in power force others to do what only they wish. They deny their victims the right to negotiate or find relief from injustice.

Repression

Sometimes people who are oppressed or exploited try to raise their heads and bring about their freedom, but they are often repressed. Those in power accuse them of planting seeds of disorder and of placing the economy and the country in danger. They do everything possible to keep the downtrodden from feeling justified in their rebellion.

Divisions

Divisions spring up all over the world among countries and peoples, especially when some appear to have everything and others have nothing! Rebellion seems inevitable in the midst of injustice. Yet, the best way of avoiding division is to work together to create an economic and political system that assures the common good, personal liberty, and sincere respect for every human being.

The Lord of Justice

Where is God?
You search for him?
You want to meet him?

He is in the pages
of his word, the Bible.
Rescuing his children
always at the right time,
from deadly enemies.

He was with
the Israelites in Egypt,
with Noah's family
on the ark, with Stephen
when the
mob stoned him. He is
alive and watching.

Where is God?
He is there,
where human beings
are in danger
and oppressed.

Places of Prayer

Since the beginning, man has had within him a knowledge of God. In fact, Solomon himself wrote that God has put eternity in the hearts of humans. We know there is someone higher than us, more intelligent, loving, and just. From Adam and Eve's rebellion to the great city states of Sumeria that housed temples to manmade gods, humans have been held captive by

Alignment of the open-air standing stones in Carnac (France)

sin. Some find the true God, while others reject him. The world is littered with the ruins of ancient religious shrines, all of whom show that people want to fill the emptiness in their hearts. Canaanite worship sites for gods and goddesses, Roman and Greek pantheons of gods, and the sun temples of South America all mark man's tragic time on earth.

The Jews

Synagogue of Ba'ram (Israel)

The Temple Solomon built in Jerusalem no longer exists. It was destroyed in 586 B.C. by the Babylonians, rebuilt and then destroyed in A.D. 70 by the Romans. Today Jews gather in synagogues (meeting places) around the world. The word "synagogue" refers both to the group that uses it and the meeting place where they gather to pray and study. Synagogues are found wherever there are faithful communities of Jews. In general the buildings face Jerusalem, the place of the original Temple. Within each synagogue, there is a sacred place, a kind of cupboard where the Torah Scroll is kept. Synagogues serve as a place of prayer and for religious education and gathering.

The Temple Mount

In Jerusalem, on the Temple Mount, where God once lived among his people, there is friction as people from various religions try to gain control of the site. The Moslem Dome of the Rock is a golden-domed structure that draws thousands of worshippers daily. Sadly, these people do not believe that Jesus Christ is God, who came to save man. The Temple Mount today is a place of sorrow, but good news: Jesus is coming back!

Mosque of Omar or the Dome of Jerusalem

Christians

Christians – whether Catholic, Orthodox, or Protestant – gather in churches. Of many varieties, churches range in size from little village churches to large cathedrals. Some are very simple with few furnishings, while others house magnificent religious art and ornate symbols of our Christian faith. Somewhere near the top of Christian churches you will usually see a cross, which is there to symbolize the Christian faith in Jesus Christ, Son of God, who rose on the third day after his death on a cross. Many churches face the east and the rising of the sun, a symbol of the Gospels light to the world. The bell tower of a church points toward heaven, and their chimes call the faithful to prayer.

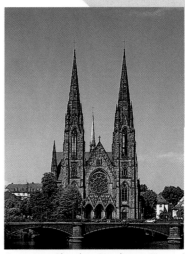

Protestant Church in Strasbourg (France)

Shrines

Around the world, people have erected shrines to many false gods. Here worshippers appeal to gods they have made from their imaginations! This is what God warned the Israelites not to do, and we can read the sad results in the Old Testament books — even in the writings of a once-wise man like Solomon.

False gods

In places like the Far East, people believe that their shrines are tied to the "divinity of nature." These shrines are positioned to be in harmony with forests, mountains, and islands. God, however, tells us that he made the natural beauty of the earth, and so we are to worship him rather than his creation.

Shrine of Miyajima (Japan)

And you,
Do you know the places of prayer in
your city, neighborhood or village?

Titles already published:

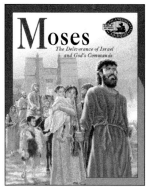
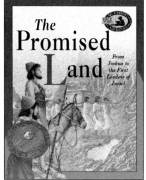

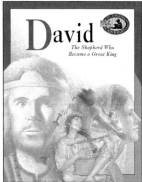
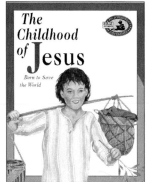
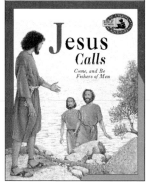
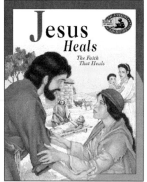

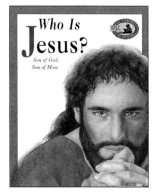
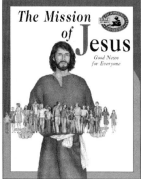
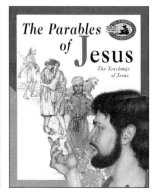

Forthcoming titles in the JUNIOR BIBLE Collection:

- The First Prophets
- Passion and Resurrection
- Exile and Return
- Isaiah, Micah, Jeremiah
- Jesus and the Outcasts
- Jesus in Jerusalem
- Acts
- Wisdom
- Psalms
- Women
- Revelation
- Letters

Solomon's Temple

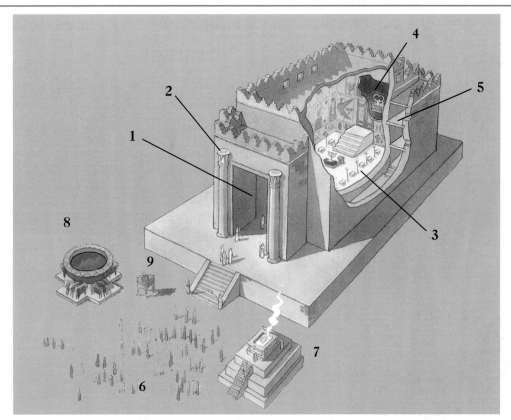

Solomon's Temple was built on a hill in the north part of Jerusalem on a huge flat foundation. The building is in the shape of a rectangle and is composed of three rooms arranged in a row.

The porch (1) separates the holy place from the steps. At each side of the entrance are *two bronze columns* of beautiful design (2). The second room is *the Holy Place* (3). It is a large room set aside for worship and offering sacrifices. It houses a large golden altar for incense, as well as tables for the bread of offering and the ten candles. Natural light pours in from high windows. The third and most sacred part of the Temple is *the Most Holy Place* (4). It is where the Sacred Chest housing the Ten Commandments rests under the outspread wings of two heavenly figures called cherubim. It is considered the throne of God. The Temple is surrounded by *three floors of chambers* (5) which were the sleeping quarters for the priests and servants of the sanctuary. Behind the building extends *a platform* (6) where the people gather. *The altar of sacrifice* (7) plays a very important role in the worship of the people. *The Sea* (8) is an enormous bronze bowl basin supported by twelve bronze bulls' heads. It contains thousands of gallons of water used for cleansing and purification during the religious ceremonies. *Ten smaller bronze bowls* (9) are placed on chariots to carry the water wherever it may be needed.

Solomon

ORIGINAL TEXT BY

Meredith HARTMAN, Karim BERRADA,

Loretta PASTVA, SND,

Albert HARI, Charles SINGER

ENGLISH TEXT ADAPTED BY

the American Bible Society

PHOTOGRAPHY

Frantisek ZVARDON, Patrice THÉBAULT,

René MATTÈS

ILLUSTRATORS

Mariano VALSESIA, Betti FERRERO

MIA. Milan Illustrations Agency

LAYOUT

Bayle Graphic Studio

FIRST PRINTING: NOVEMBER 2000

Copyright © 2000 by Master Books
for the CBA U.S. edition.

For information write: Master Books, P.O. Box 727, Green Forest, AR 72638.

ISBN: 0-89051-332-5

ÉDITIONS
DU SIGNE
© ÉDITIONS DU SIGNE 1997